Rubik's Cube

The complete guide

for beginners

Damiano Bacchin

Copyright © 2020 Damiano Bacchin

All Rights Reserved

ISBN 9798646570056

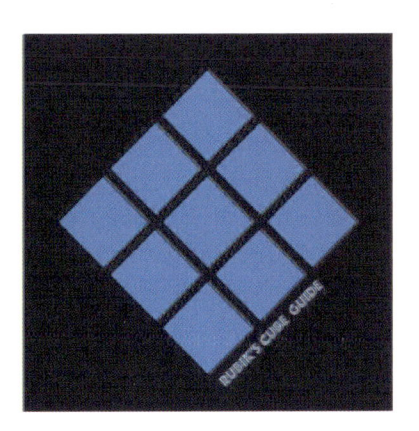

Follow **@the.ultimate.cuber.guide** for more guides

INDEX

	Introduction	7
Step 1	The white cross	11
Step 2	The white face	15
Step 3	The second layer	18
Step 4	The yellow cross	22
Step 5	The yellow face	24
Step 6	Permuting the corners	27
Step 7	Permuting the edges	29
Bonus	Creating patterns	35

INTRODUCTION

Welcome!

You're trying to solve that enigmatic colorful toy, but you don't know where to start. You're able to complete one colored side, but, as soon as you try to solve the others, you mess up everything you've just done. You found thousands of methods on the internet, but you don't understand those complicated annotations.

Stop worrying: you're in the right place! This guide will teach you how to solve the Rubik's cube entirely in a quick and easy way. You don't need any special abilities to solve it, it's a game made for everyone, such as kids and adults who want to keep their minds well-trained.

The method is really simple but, in case you don't understand something or if you need help, you can always rely on my support (at the end of the book you'll find an e-mail address to which I will reply personally to clarify any doubts).

WHAT YOU'RE GOING TO FIND IN THIS MANUAL

In this book you will find a *step-by-step* guide on how to solve the cube applying the easiest methods in existence. There are pictures and descriptions, thanks to which you'll learn the main resolution strategies and all the possible cases you could encounter.

You won't find any complicated sequences of alphanumeric codes that other guides suggest, but you're going to learn everything through simple images that will illustrate the moves to make.

HOW TO READ THIS BOOK

As strange as it may seem, I'd like to make a clarification about the way you should approach this method. It is important to try to follow the guide step by step, without rushing to solve the cube in one go, giving you the right amount of time to assimilate every single step's strategies and moves. The one thing you must avoid is reading the whole book first and then trying to apply the method later: this is not only useless, but it can also be counterproductive, since it could create a lot of confusion.

WHAT YOU WILL GET FROM THIS GUIDE

My goal is to teach you the easiest way to solve the Rubik's cube independently, without the need to rely on any guide to check the moves every time. Remember that this is the easiest way, not the fastest! However, after a little bit of practice, you should be able to solve the cube in less than 90 seconds, I can assure you.

BEFORE STARTING

First of all, I find it useful to make a clarification about some of the technical data by providing some useful information on the Rubik's cube.

The Magic Cube (as it was originally named by its creator, Erno Rubik, a Hungarian architect) is a famous riddle that won't need any greater introductions: it consists of a cube with six faces marked in different colors, composed of smaller cubes (called *cubelets*) arranged in threes on every side of the cube, held together by a central mechanism, which allows every face of the cube to rotate independently.

It is for this reason that there are so many ways to scramble the cube, specifically 43.252.003.274.489.856.000 combinations (I'll spare you the calculation of the needed combinations to achieve this result). It is an impressive number: you're already asking yourself "how am I going to know how to solve each of these combinations?!"

You don't need to worry at all because, as you go along with the cube's solving, the possible number of combinations will drastically decrease, until you reach the final step that, for example, only allows two of them.

Is everything clear so far? Great, let's move on!

How many *cubelets* does a Rubik's cube contain? You would guess 27: each side of the cube has got 3 cubelets so 3×3×3 = 27. Actually, every cube has got 26 cubelets, since the center is occupied by the *core*, the mechanism that holds every piece together making them slide amongst each other.

Now, let's analyze the three types of *cubelets*:

CENTERS

Centers are 6 (one for each face), they've got just one color and they're fixed between them, in the sense that their mutual position never changes, whatever move you make: the couples of opposite centers will always be white-yellow, green-blue, red-orange. Seeing is believing!

Thanks to this piece of information, we can deduce that the centers determine the face's color. When, for example, I'll tell you to look for the red face when the cube is in a messy order, you're going to look for the red center and you'll know that all the other red pieces have to be put in that red face.

EDGES

Edges are 12 and they've got 2 colors, because they're on the line between 2 faces. For each position they occupy, they've got two arrangements (for ex. yellow-green and green-yellow). Keep this in mind when we're going to solve the cube.

CORNERS

Corners are 8 and they've got 3 colors, because they're in the line between 3 faces. Every position includes different possible arrangements, same as the edges, in this case they're three.

The colors of the faces that I'll be taking into consideration in this guide are white-yellow, green-blue, red-orange because they're the most used colors in the vast majority of the cubes (as the original one). Other types of cubes with slightly different colors or disposed in a different order are on the market, especially the older ones. In that case you don't have to worry. The method works just as fine; you only need to take differences into account. You can check the colors arrangements of your cube simply looking at the centers.

Good, now we're ready to start solving the first step.

STEP 1

THE WHITE CROSS

As you can see from the image above, the first step is to create a white cross inserting the white edges on the face where the white center is. Remember there are four edges with the white color (white-red, white-green, white-orange, white-blue) and each of them has got different colors, so we need to be careful when inserting the white edges on the white face in order to also match the colors on the lateral sides.

To make sure we insert the white edges in the right way, we will put them all in the yellow face (the one with the yellow center, standing on the opposite face compared to the white one) and then we will put them in the white face, making sure that the lateral colors match. So, in this first step you won't need to look at the second color of the white edges.

Let's see how to do it.

First of all, I suggest you to hold the cube with both hands in front of you, so that the yellow center is at the top (and therefore the white center is going to be at the bottom) and the other colors (blue, orange, green and red) will be sideways.

CASE 1

The easiest case is when a white edge is on the side faces: simply rotate the face it's on to side the yellow center.

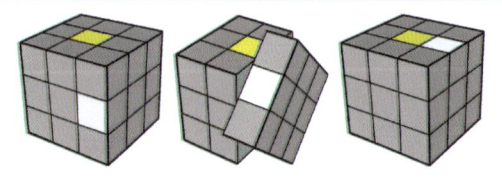

CASE 2

If the insertion of the edge undoes another edge previously inserted in the yellow face, simply rotate the yellow face until the position where the new edge will be put is free.

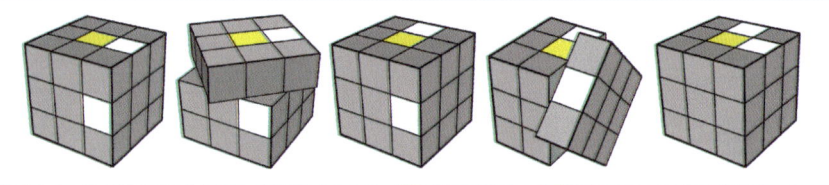

CASE 3

In case the edge is on the lateral faces, but at the top or at the bottom, first you have to rotate the face where it is located to position it in the right way, transforming it in a case 1 or 2.

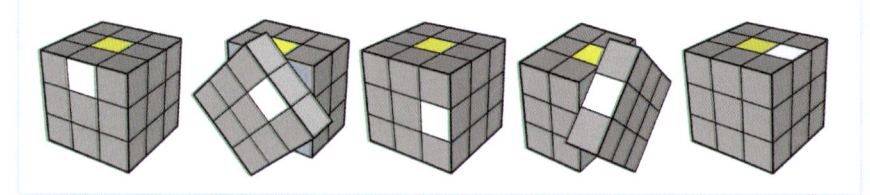

CASE 4

Now let's see the last case you can possibly find.

When the white edge is at the bottom, on the white face (indicated by the little arrow in the figure below), you have to rotate the face until the space above will be free and then turn the face where the piece is twice.

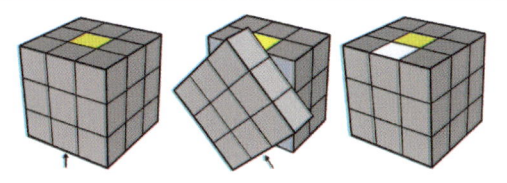

By repeating this procedure for all the white edges, making sure not to undo the edges already done while inserting a new one (as explained in case 2), at some point you should get to a flower-like shape (a white cross with the yellow center, as shown in the figure on the right).

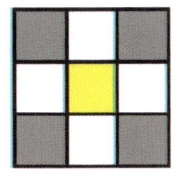

At this point we are ready to insert the white edges on the white face, which is located just below. To do this, you need to choose an edge from those inserted (for example, let's take the white-green edge); after choosing it, we must rotate the yellow face until the lateral color of the chosen edge matches the color of the respective center.

Once the edge is coupled with its center, it is possible to insert it into the white face by twisting the face of the center of that color twice. Keeping the same example, once the white-green edge is coupled with the green center, just rotate the green face twice.

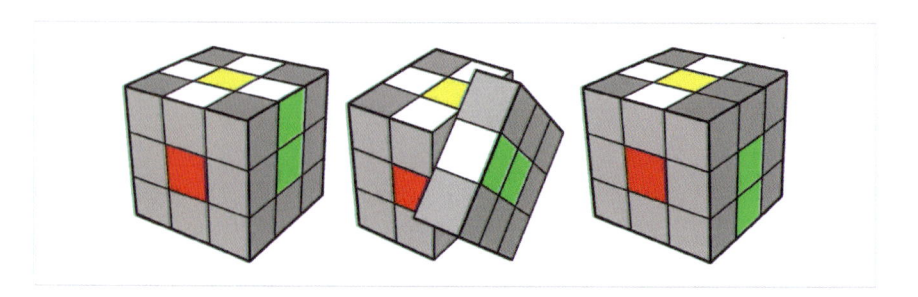

Repeat the operation with the other white edges left in the yellow face: choose a color from the rest, rotate the yellow face until the color of that edge is coupled with its center, insert it in the white face by twisting the face of the color of the edge twice. In some cases, the edges will already be coupled with their centers: just insert them by turning the colored face twice.

As soon as you have repeated the operation for all the edges, you will have formed a white cross in the bottom face with the edges in the right positions, i.e. coupled with the respective centers, as shown in the image at the beginning of the chapter (only upside down, just keep holding the cube with yellow on top and white on bottom).

STEP 2

THE WHITE FACE

In this second step we will complete the white face by inserting the corners that contain the white color.

Always keeping the cube with the white face down, we must look for the white corners in the upper layer (in the image below I highlighted in blue the layer in which you have to look for the white pieces. Attention: do not consider the face on the top, the yellow one, but only the highlighted band): these are going to be the first ones to be inserted.

The other positions where the white corners may be located are in the yellow face at the top, or in the first layer. We will deal with these latter two cases later.

You then choose a white corner located in the upper layer and rotate the yellow face until we bring it exactly above the place where it should be inserted. I must remind you that the corners have three colors: in order to see which position a corner will be inserted, just look at the colors of the faces (in the example I use the white-red-green edge: you will see that I positioned it exactly above the place that it should be inserted).

Hold the cube so that the angle you have chosen is right in front of you: you should be able to see the top face and two side faces, as shown in the figures below.

At this point there can be two cases: if the white piece is on the right side, follow the first scheme; if the white piece, on the other hand, is on the left side, follow the second scheme.

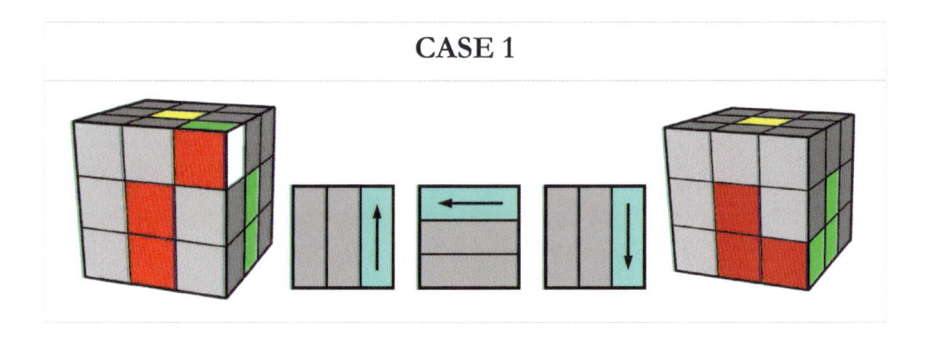

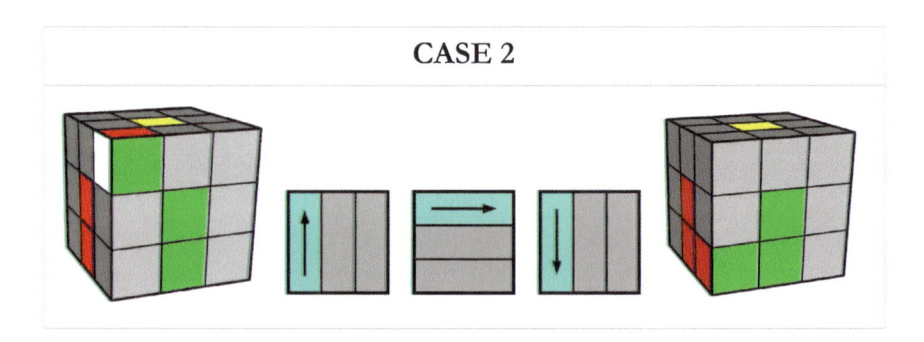

CASE 1

CASE 2

Once you have inserted this first corner, choose another one in the last layer and repeat the mechanism: rotate the yellow face until you have brought it over its place, see if it is to the right or left and perform one of the two schemes.

When you are finished inserting the white corners in the last layer, let's see how to insert those in the other positions.

If the white piece is located in the yellow face at the top, we must make sure to bring it in the band of the upper layer (the one highlighted in blue). To do this, we insert it with one of the two schemes indicated above but, since it was rotated, we will realize that we entered it incorrectly. At this point we will have to "pull it out" by inserting another random corner with *the same pattern* as earlier (for example, if to insert it I used the right pattern, to pull it out I will need to insert another at random using always the right pattern).

This way our angle should now be in the top layer, ready to be correctly inserted (using scheme 1 or 2).

If, on the other hand, the white corner is in the lower layer, but not correctly inserted, simply "pull it out" by inserting a random corner performing one of the two left/right patterns. Once pulled out, you can reconnect to the cases already described above to insert it correctly.

After repeating these procedures for all four corners, you will have completed the white face and all the first layer correctly, as shown in the photo at the beginning of the chapter (upside down, in order to let you see the white face well).

Congratulations! :D

STEP 3

THE SECOND LAYER

Up till this point the cube could be solved in an "intuitive" way, with attempts, without using precise algorithms or schemes. For this, I advise you to experiment with your personal technique, using the moves you feel most comfortable with.

From now on, however, it will be more difficult to go on inserting the pieces without undoing what we have already done, therefore we will need *algorithms*. The word may frighten you, but you need to know that the algorithms are nothing more than sequences of moves that allow you to modify a part of the cube without undoing the already resolved part.

We immediately begin to see the first algorithm, which allows us to insert the edges from the upper layer to the second layer.

We already know that the edges that contain the yellow color will go to the top layer, so in this step we will have to ignore them. Let's focus on what we need to insert: green-orange, orange-blue, blue-red, red-green.

Choose one of these in the last layer and turn the yellow face until the lateral color of this edge coincides with the color of the center. Let's keep the face with the coupled edge-center in front of us and see which side we will have to insert our edge: the two possibilities are left and right.

Here are the algorithms that you will have to apply to solve these two cases:

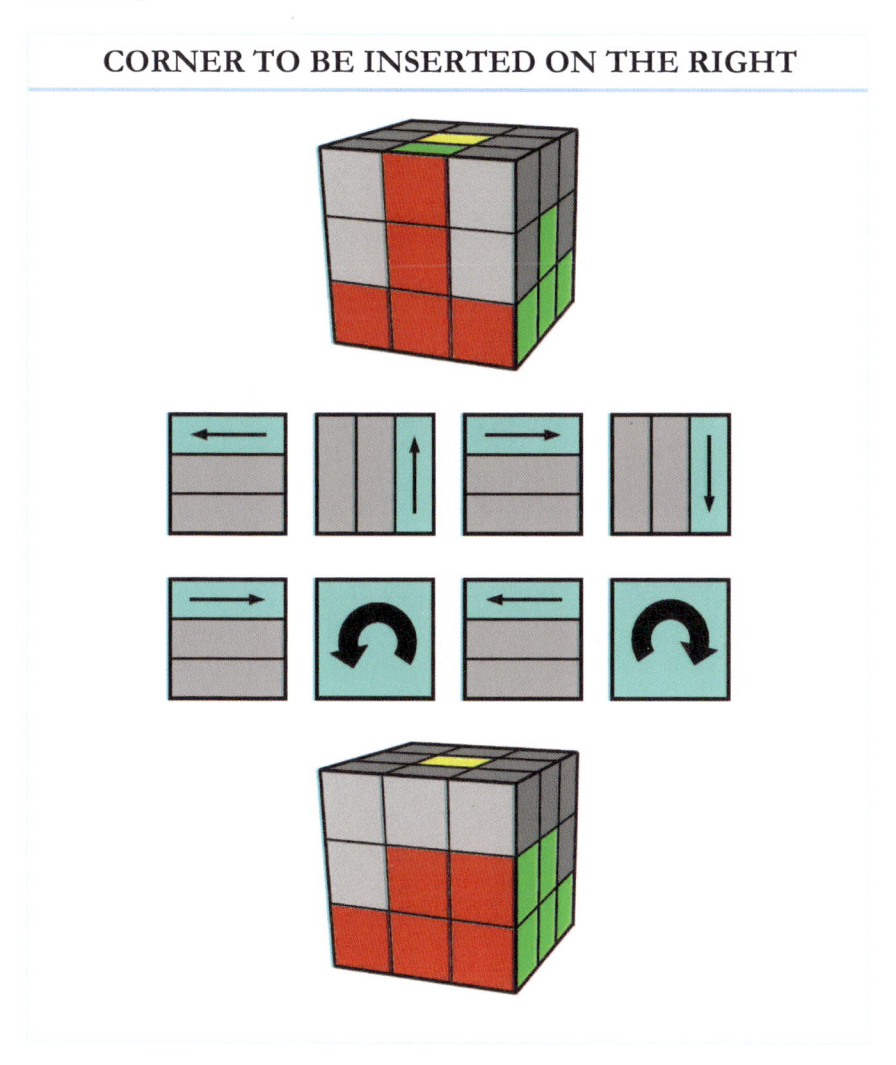

CORNER TO BE INSERTED ON THE RIGHT

The sixth and eighth moves of the algorithm (those colored in green, with the circular arrow) represent a rotation of the front face which, in the example, is the red one.

CORNER TO BE INSERTED ON THE LEFT

What if there are no more corners in the last layer? If you have not finished the second yet and you no longer have pieces in the last layer to insert, it means that the "good" edges are already inserted in the second layer, but in the wrong way, they are crooked or have changed position, for example. To continue, just insert, applying one of the two algorithms described above, a random corner in place of one of the "good" corners inserted incorrectly, so as you "pull it out". Once this is done, your "good" edge will be in the third layer, ready to be inserted correctly, as already explained.

At this point you should have managed to complete the entire second layer of the cube. A great satisfaction, isn't it?

I remind you that if you're having a hard time with something, any at all or some passages are not clear to you, or for any other need for that matter, you can safely contact me at my email address:

rubiks.cube.official.guide@gmail.com

I will be happy to answer you as soon as possible.

STEP 4

THE YELLOW CROSS

At this point, the next moves you will make will be aimed at completing the yellow face. How do you do it? Let's start by making a yellow cross, then insert all the yellow edges.

Once the second layer is complete, look at the yellow face at the top. There are three different cases that you could encounter, please look at the image below.

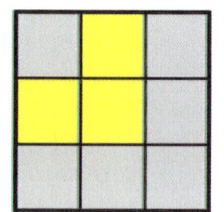

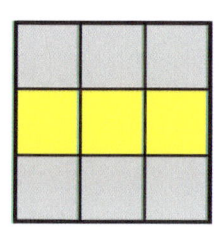

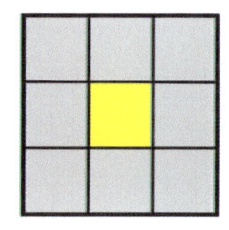

I would like to point out that only the positions of the yellow edges count in this step. For now, you don't have to consider the angles, so focus on identifying the three cases only taking into account the edges.

All you have to do is orientate the cube so you can see one of the three cases indicated above, always keep it with the yellow face on top, then you will apply this easy algorithm:

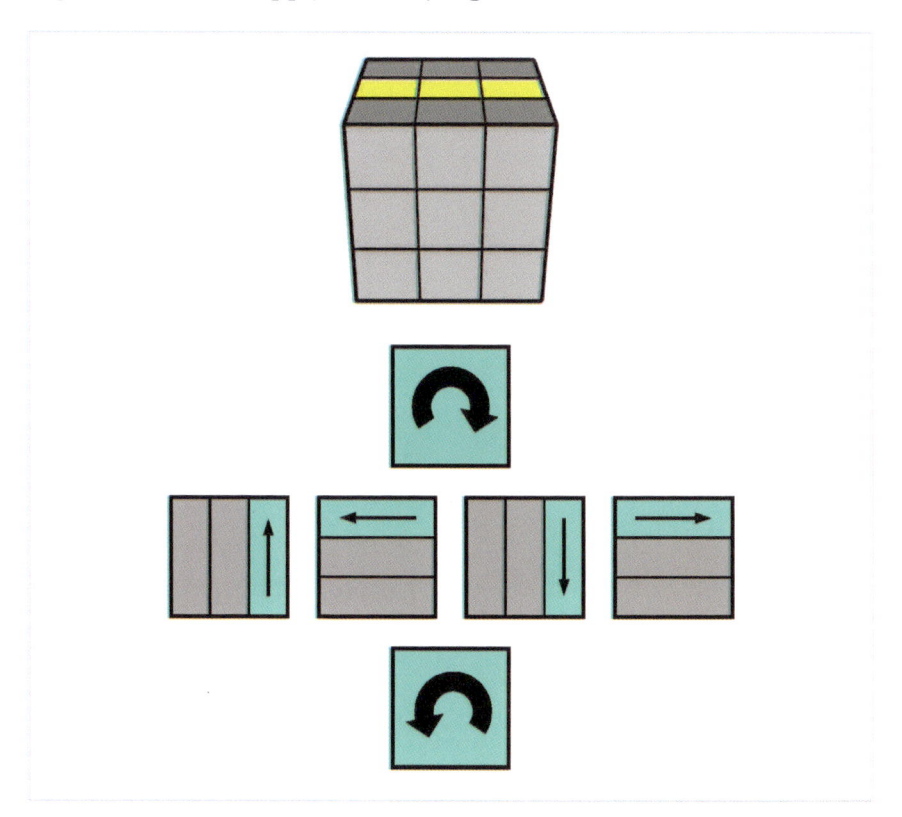

If the configuration you had before running the algorithm was a line yellow horizontal, your yellow cross should already have appeared. If you had that L upside down figure, you have obtained the horizontal line and you just need to repeat the algorithm. If instead you started from the configuration with only the yellow center, you will have to repeat the algorithm more times and each of these times you will fall back in one of the two previous cases.

If you notice that the side colors of the edges do not match the centers of the side faces (green, red, blue, orange) do not worry, since we are going to fix them in the last step. For now, the important thing is that you can see the yellow cross on the face at the top.

STEP 5

THE YELLOW FACE

To complete the yellow face, all that remains to do is orienting the yellow corners all upwards. After completing the yellow cross, you may encounter 7 cases (actually there would be 8: the eighth case is the yellow face already solved ... it can happen, but it is quite rare); don't worry, all you need is an algorithm to solve them all.

You can see the first 6 cases below:

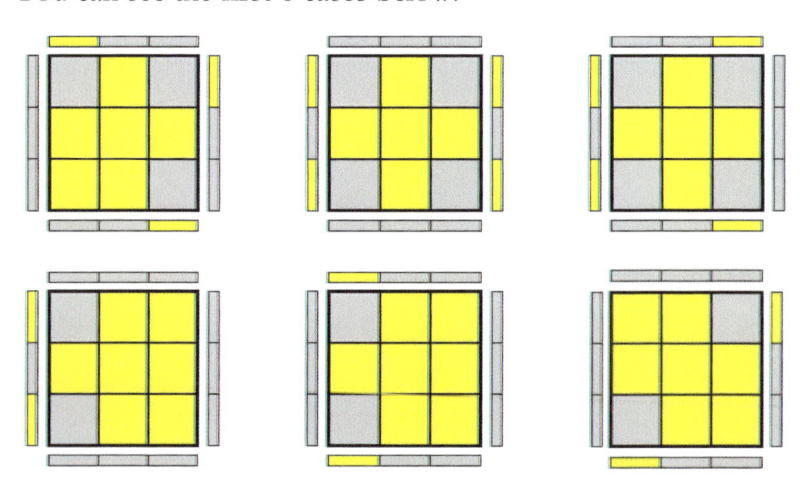

The figures also show the yellow pieces on the side faces.

Use the following algorithm (called Sune) being careful to orient the cube correctly, as shown in the examples above. (The example shows how to orient the cube in the first of the 6 cases).

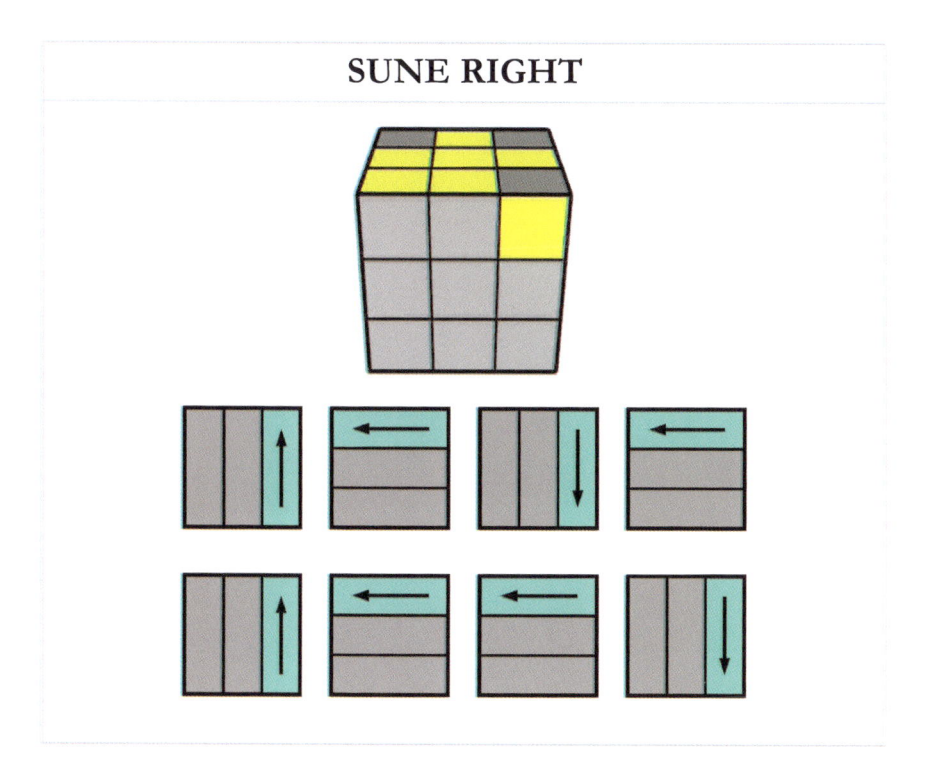

SUNE RIGHT

In this example you can see how the algorithm directly solves the first of these 6 cases. What about the other 5? Running the algorithm after having properly oriented the cube, you will fall back to the first case and you will just have to repeat the same algorithm. If by chance you have oriented the cube incorrectly, after performing the Sune, instead of falling back in case 1 or ending the yellow face, you will fall in another case and you will have to repeat the Sune again.

Now let's see the last case, case 7. You will find that it is the mirror of case 1, therefore to solve it you just need to perform the algorithm in a mirror way!

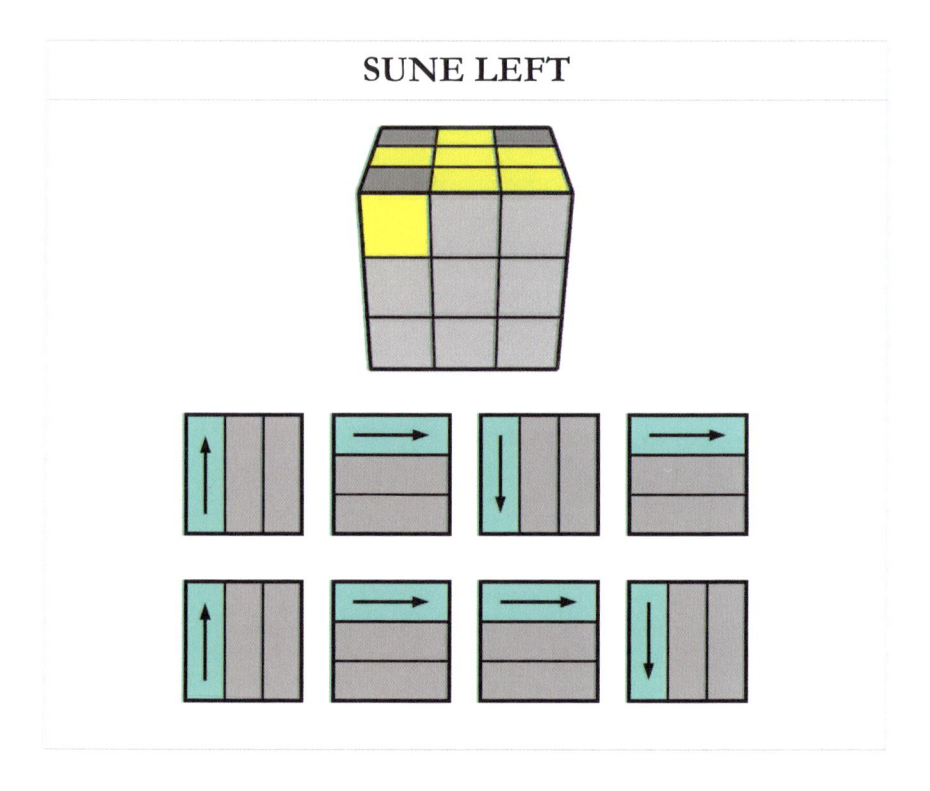

SUNE LEFT

By applying this algorithm, a maximum of two times, you will be able to complete the yellow face, as shown at the beginning of the chapter.

Now we begin to see a certain order in the cube, don't we? Be brave, we are almost at the end!

STEP 6

CORNERS OF THE LAST LAYER

At this point the cube will appear practically solved, if it weren't for the third layer. In this step we will then reorder the corners by swapping their positions so that the colors match the other faces. This "exchange of positions" between the pieces is called *permutation*.

About 80% of the time, you will find in the last layer at least a pair of corners of the same color on the same face, as shown in the figure.

When this happens, you will have to hold the face with the pair of corners to the left (always yellow face at the top) and apply the following algorithm.

PERMUTATION OF THE EDGES

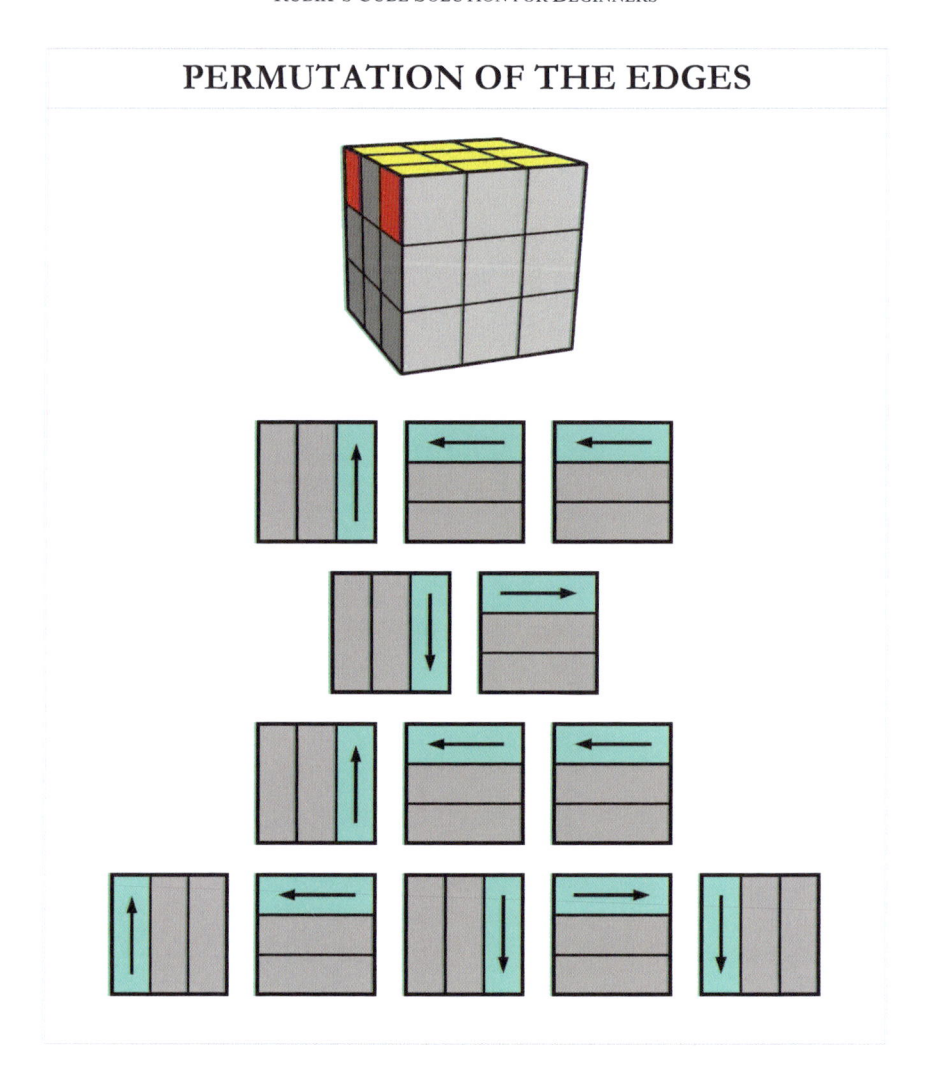

In 20% of the cases, you won't find any pair of angles with the same color on the same face, so you just need to perform the algorithm with any orientation. After doing this, double-check the corners: you will find a pair. Run the algorithm, after properly orienting the cube, and here you will have permuted the corners of the last layer.

What is missing now to complete the cube? We need to permute the third layer edges! However, we will see this in the next chapter.

STEP 7

THE EDGES OF THE LAST LAYER

Let's observe the two possible cases:

1. An edge is in the correct position; the other three edges are exchanged.
2. All four edges are exchanged in position.

Now let's see how to solve case 1.

Hold the cube so that the yellow face is at the top and the face with the corner inserted correctly (which will be completed) is behind it. The faces in the front, right and left will have the wrong edges of the last layer. To fix them, you will first have to see if the edges will be fixed by turning them clockwise or counterclockwise.

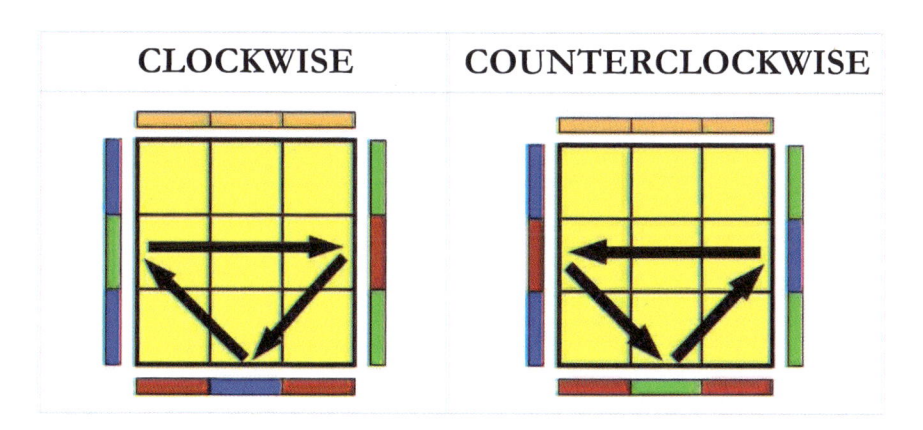

CLOCKWISE	**COUNTERCLOCKWISE**

Now we're going to see the procedure we need to rotate the edges in these two cases.

Three steps are required, to be performed in order. If the edges have to turn counterclockwise, you will perform the right Sune, then you will orient the cube and conclude with the left Sune.

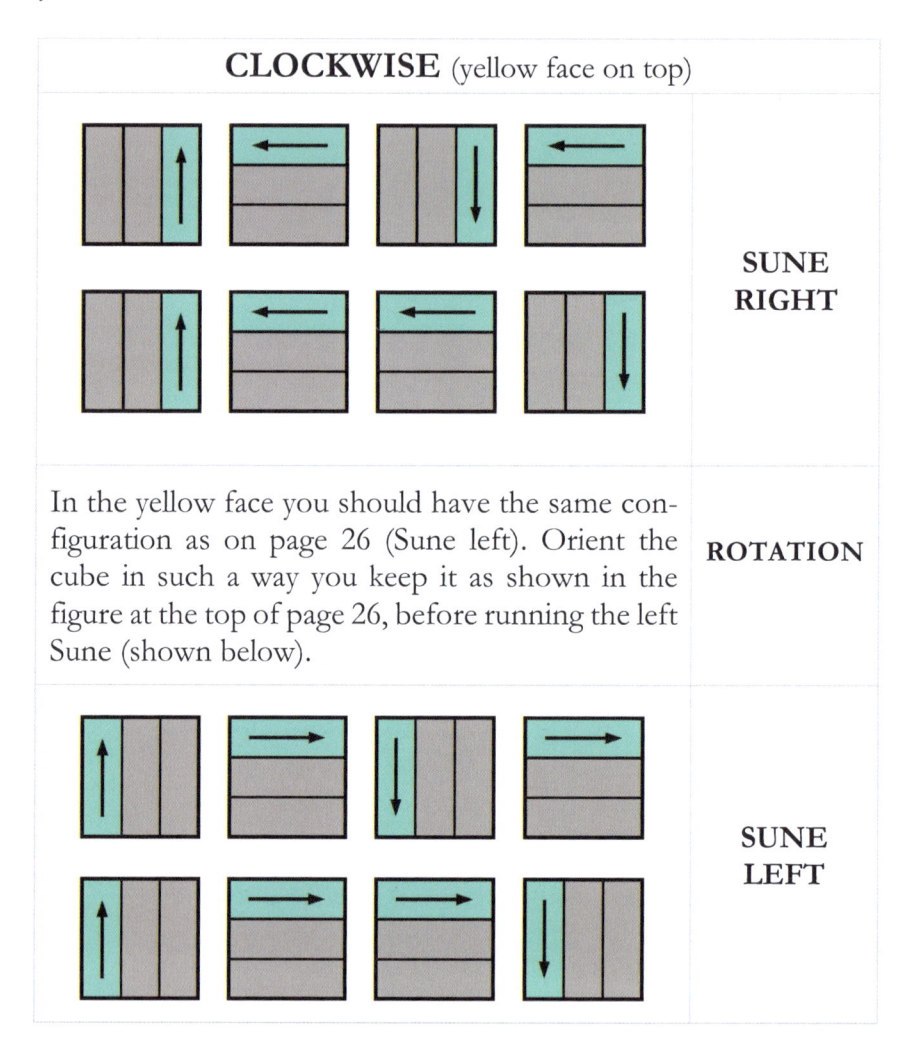

CLOCKWISE (yellow face on top)	
	SUNE RIGHT
In the yellow face you should have the same configuration as on page 26 (Sune left). Orient the cube in such a way you keep it as shown in the figure at the top of page 26, before running the left Sune (shown below).	**ROTATION**
	SUNE LEFT

COUNTERCLOCKWISE (yellow face on top)

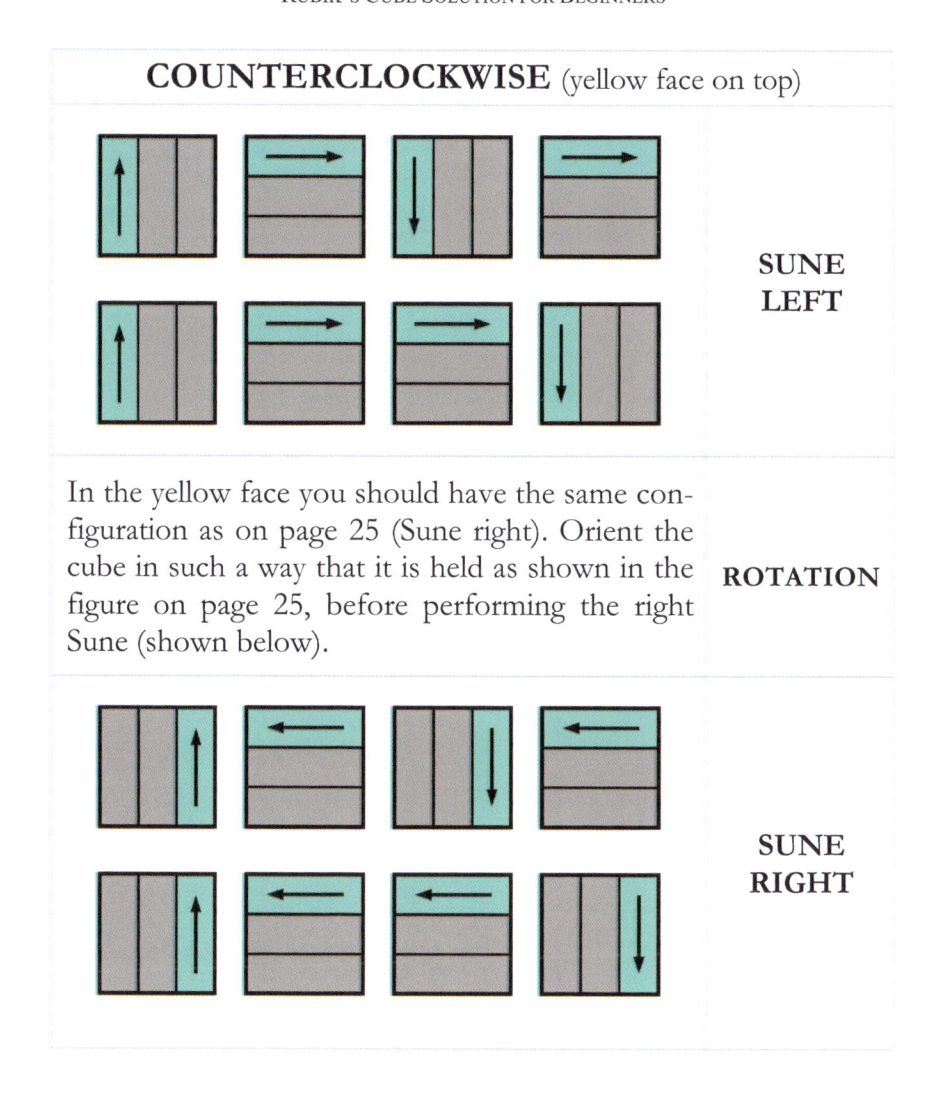

SUNE LEFT

In the yellow face you should have the same configuration as on page 25 (Sune right). Orient the cube in such a way that it is held as shown in the figure on page 25, before performing the right Sune (shown below).

ROTATION

SUNE RIGHT

If, instead, all four edges of the last layer were in the wrong position, just apply one of the two sequences (clockwise or counterclockwise) and you will fall back in one of the two cases, clockwise or counterclockwise.

Congratulations!

If you managed to solve the Rubik's cube thanks to this guide,
your review on Amazon would be very welcome.

If some passages are not clear to you and you would like it to be explained better, do not hesitate to contact me!

rubiks.cube.official.guide@gmail.com

FINAL CONSIDERATIONS

Now that you have managed to solve the cube for the first time, it is important to do it and undo it over and over again, in order to be able to experiment with all of the combinations.

When you are familiar with the method, you can begin to memorize one step at a time: first learn the different cases that you might encounter in that step, the consequent solution strategies and finally the algorithms. After a little practice you should be able to solve the cube entirely, without needing to check this guide anymore.

Another improvement you could make, once you master the "basic" method, is to try and improve your resolution time. For this goal you will need: a cube for *speedcubing*, the right technique to move the faces with your fingers (through the so-called *fingertricks*) and advanced algorithms that will save you many moves.

All this useful information will be available in my next book, which I will release shortly.

If you want to receive an e-mail as soon as the next book is available on Amazon, ask me at my e-mail address.

Thanks for choosing this book,
Until next time, have fun!

BONUS

CREATING FANTASTIC PATTERNS WITH THE CUBE

In this last chapter I will teach you how to create fantastic patterns after you have solved the cube.

In this section, when you find this move ⟳ or its symmetrical one, you will have to rotate the face behind, following the arrow direction. Be careful not to confuse them with this ⟳ and its symmetrical one, where instead you will need to rotate the front face.

Since the starting configuration is the solved cube, you can keep whatever orientation as you like while carrying out these algorithms. By changing the orientation, the colors with which the patterns will be created will also change.

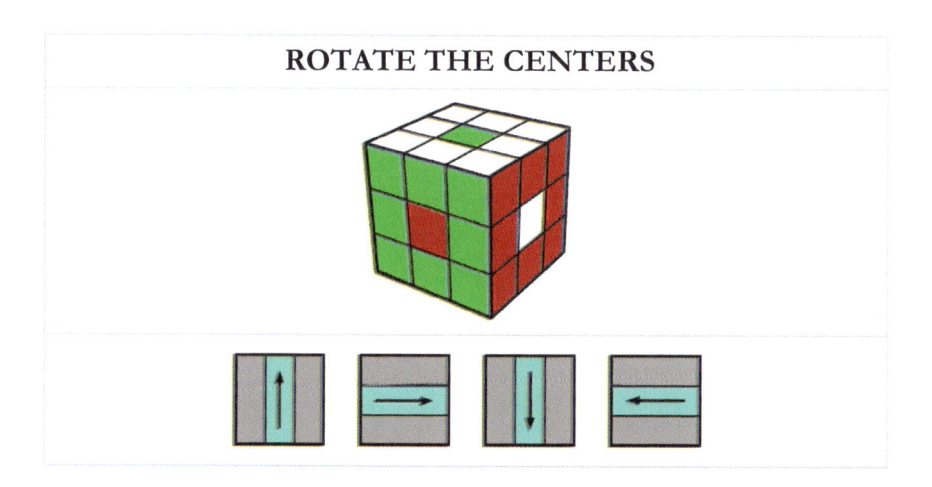

ROTATE THE CENTERS

CHESSBOARD

Per ottenere questa configurazione, ti basterà ruotare due volte (quindi di 180°) tutte e sei le facce del cubo.

CUBE IN A CUBE

ANACONDA

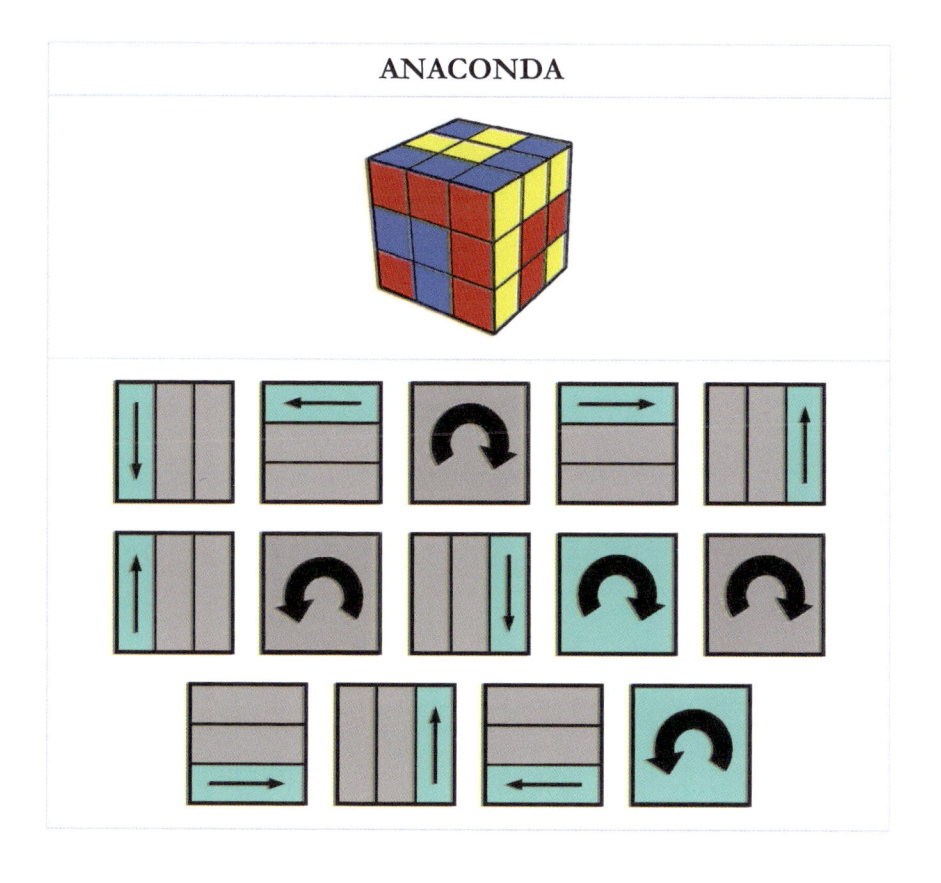

For more patterns, follow me on Instagram

@the.ultimate.cuber.guide

Printed in Great Britain
by Amazon